1

Knowledge Books and

Hi, I am Trevor Fourmile, proud Yidinji man. Art is a very big part of my culture. It has been important to us for thousands of years. Our First Nations people were storytellers. They did not use writing to tell their stories. They told them orally. They told them through dance, and they told them through their art. Come and find out more about the meaning of the artwork in my poem, *The Colour Ochre Warrior*.

Knowledge Books and Software

3

The Yidinji people were great warriors. The shield was very important to them. There were many different types of shields. This one was called Bigun. It was made from the slippery, blue fig tree. Bigun was used for protection, and to carry fruit and berries. It was also a place to display totems.

Knowledge Books and Software

5

The warriors of my clan used to paint themselves with a lawyer cane design. The cane is used for food, as a paint brush, for making traps, and for shelter. The leaves are used for the outer layer of the hut. They were also used to make a skirt or a cassowary dance decoration. The white colour in the middle is the main ochre used for dancing.

Knowledge Books and Software

7

Knowledge Books and Software

The blue, red, and yellow are the colours of the cassowary neck. The feathers of the cassowary are shown in black. The cassowary is the giver of life in Yidinji culture. It eats and spreads the seeds of the rainforest trees. This makes more shade, food, and shelter for the Yidinji people. Without the cassowary, the rainforest wouldn't exist.

Knowledge Books and Software

9

This art shows a journey of healing. The dark circle shows someone who is lost and feeling sad. After their journey back home, they have reconnected with country and are feeling better. Yidinji people believe in walking barefoot and digging our feet in the ground when we go home. This lets the Spirits and energy from Mother Earth enter our body.

Knowledge Books and Software

Can you also see the Southern Cross in this art? The stars were very important to my people. They used them on their journeys to find their way back home. These stars are called Bijugan.

Knowledge Books and Software

Mugaru is a fish trap that is shaped like a butterfly. Girrway is a fish net that was sewn together. This art shows the beautiful design. Can you also see the water symbol? It flows along with the stitches that hold the net together.

15

In Yidinji culture, Bana is water. It is the giver of life. In Far North Queensland, it rains a lot. Sometimes it can cause very fast running water. This is called Danggay.

Knowledge Books and Software

It is very important for our people to reconnect to our country. These journeys help to heal us. The patterns are like clouds. They show the changes and challenges that we face in life. The footprints in between show the journey that we take.

Knowledge Books and Software

Knowledge, ideas and software

The Black Bean and the Match Box Bean are found along the blue water of the riverbeds. You must prepare them well before eating them. The shell is used for necklaces or decoration. They are also used to make music. The poison can be taken from the seed and used to help catch fish. These rainforest trees have many uses!

Knowledge Books and Software

21

During springtime, you can see these Gingaa caterpillars moving along the ground like a long freight train. Warriors rubbed the Gingaa poison onto their spear tips for hunting. When the caterpillars started moving, the Yidinji people knew that winter was on its way. Next time you are looking at art, look very closely - you're sure to find messages everywhere!

Knowledge Books and Software

Knowle... and Software

Word bank

Yidinji	cassowary	beautiful
culture	decoration	design
important	ochre	symbol
thousands	exist	Bana
storytellers	journey	Danggay
orally	reconnected	challenges
Bigun	energy	decoration
slippery	Bijugan	Gingaa
protection	Mugaru	caterpillars
totems	Girrway	
lawyer	sewn	

Knowledge Books and Software